THE AMERICAN NEGRO

HIS HISTORY AND LITERATURE

FROM SLAVERY
TO THE BISHOPRIC
IN THE A. M. E. CHURCH

William H. *enry* Heard

ARNO PRESS and THE NEW YORK TIMES
NEW YORK 1969

General Editor
WILLIAM LOREN KATZ

In 1908 a former slave, William Henry Heard (1850–1937), became the thirty-fifth bishop of the African Methodist Episcopal Church, the oldest Negro denomination in America. In 1924 he published a brief autobiography, *From Slavery to the Bishopric in the A. M. E. Church.* His narrative provides an insight into the lives of black Americans over a seventy-five-year span, and shows the workings of the most significant Afro-American church.

Unfortunately, Bishop Heard divided his autobiography into topical chapters dealing successively with his birth, slavery, education, politics, travel, conversion, ministry, and bishopric; the last (ninth) chapter discusses those persons, such as Frederick Douglass, who influenced him personally. Each chapter retraces the story of his life, causing overlapping and a confused chronology. And with only seventy-three pages devoted to his life, some gaps were inevitable.

Bishop Heard was born into slavery in

i

Georgia on June 25, 1850. He describes vividly the slaves' crude quarters and privation. Interestingly, his father, unlike many male slaves, was a strong father figure, a self-taught craftsman on a neighboring plantation. Heard describes his mother as a "breeder" who was given special privilegs for regularly bearing children. Her death left nine-year-old William to care for his younger sisters and brother. He was a plow-boy his last five years in slavery, escaping in 1865 when Union army troops appeared.

As a slave his education had been confined to memorizing Bible passages and catechism lessons because it was unlawful to teach slaves more than that. Determined as a freedman to secure an education, the fifteen-year-old lad scrimped from his small earnings in his father's wheelwright shop to pay barely literate whites to teach him his letters.

Active politicaly during Reconstruction, he ran for the legislature in 1868 and by 1872 was Republican Party chairman of his native county of Elbert. Meanwhile, he attended the Negro school that opened in Elberton, mastering the lessons so rapidly that he became a teacher.

From 1873 to 1877, he lived in South Carolina, teaching school in Mt. Carmel, attending the University of South Carolina for two years (while it was under carpetbagger control), and winning a seat in the legislature in 1876. The return of the Democrats to power terminated his collegiate and legislative career in South Carolina. Blacklisted as a teacher because of politics, he returned to Georgia where he found his calling.

Heard taught briefly in Athens and continued his studies at Clark and Atlanta universities. He began studying law with an attorney in Athens, but on May 16, 1879, he was converted and chose a career in the ministry. Licensed by the African Methodist Episcopal Church, he served as an exhorter and as a local preacher. In 1880, the eighth bishop of the A. M. E. Church, Jabez P. Campbell, assigned him to a mission church in Johnstown, Georgia, where he served for two years. The new bishop, William F. Dickerson, fifteenth in A .M. E. history, ordained Heard as a deacon in 1881 and as an elder two years later, assigning him to a church in Atlanta in 1882. Heard supported himself with a federal railway mail clerk job secured in 1880 as a result of aiding an Independent Democrat's campaign for Congress.

In 1883, Heard gave up his $1,150 postal job in order to devote himself full time to a pastorate in Aiken, South Carolina, at $355 a year. After two years, he was assigned to a larger, better-paying ($1,000 salary and $500 perquisites) church, Mt. Zion, in Charleston, where he served from 1885 to 1888. A vigorous pastor, he increased membership, paid off debts, and raised large sums for diocesan and mission work. Although he omits it from his autobiography, he won a suit against railroad segregation in 1887 before the new Interstate Commerce Commission.[1]

Heard moved to Philadelphia in 1888, making his home there for the remainder of his life. He served a year there at Allen Chapel, named for the founder and first bishop (1816) of the A.M.E. denomination, Richard Allen, and continued his education at Miller Memorial Theological Seminary. After Heard served a year as presiding elder of the Lancaster district, the thirteenth bishop, Henry M. Turner, assigned him to Bethel Church in Philadelphia, the denomination's mother church, founded in 1794 by Allen. In two years there, Heard built an imposing new edifice.

After three more years with churches in Delaware and Pennsylvania, he became a diplomat and missionary. From 1895 to 1899, by appointment of President Grover Cleveland, a Democrat, Heard served as United States Minister Resident and Consul General to Liberia. While there, he also served his church as Superintendent of the Liberia Conference, building the first A.M.E. church located within the capital city of Monrovia.

From 1899 to 1904, Heard served in church posts in Pennsylvania, New York, and Georgia. For the next four years, he travelled throughout the nation as Secretary-Treasurer of the A.M.E. Connectional Preachers Aid and Mutual Relief Society.

In 1908, at the General Conference in Norfolk, Heard was elected to the bishopric. As a bishop he served in West Africa, 1908–1916; the 8th Episcopal district (Mississippi and Louisiana), 1916–1920; and the 1st district (Middle

Atlantic and New England states), 1920–1937.

Active in the World Faith and Order Conference, he encountered housing discrimination when he attended the meeting in Edinburgh in August, 1937, as the oldest delegate. Sir John Simon, Chancellor of the Exchequer, and the Archbishop of York, Dr. William Temple, expressed indignation; the latter invited Bishop Heard to stay with him. The bishop declined, having found a small hotel that would accept him. The manager of the hotel that had barred him explained that Negro guests upset American tourists.[2] Three weeks after returning from Scotland in apparent good health, the bishop became ill and died on September 12, 1937.

In Bishop Heard's autobiography, we glimpse slavery, the conditions of freedmen, Reconstruction politics, and prejudice at home and abroad. We also see the career of a dedicated A.M.E. clergyman.

Edgar Allan Toppin
PROFESSOR OF HISTORY
VIRGINIA STATE COLLEGE

NOTES

1. George Brown Tindall, *South Carolina Negroes, 1877–1900* (Baton Rouge: Louisiana State University Press, 1966), p. 206; August Meier, *Negro Thought in America, 1880–1915* (Ann Arbor: University of Michigan Press, 1966), p. 72. Useful for filling out the story of Heard's life are the following biographical sketches: Richard R. Wright, Jr. and John R. Hawkins (eds.), *Centennial Encyclopaedia of the African Methodist Episcopal Church, 1816–1916* (Philadelphia: A.M.E. Book Concern, 1916), p. 111; "Obituary," *New York Times,* September 13, 1937, p. 21; and "Obituary," *Norfolk Journal and Guide,* September 18, 1937, pp. 1 and 10. These three sketches contain some errors, but the accounts in *Who Was Who In America* (1897–1942) and in *Who's Who In Colored America* (1937) contain too many errors to be of any help.

2. *New York Times,* August 8, 1937, p. 29, and August 9, 1937, p. 34. See also, Richard Bardolph, *The Negro Vanguard* (New York: Vintage, 1961), p. 159. Bardolph has a useful summary of Heard's life up to 1895 (pp. 95–96).

FROM
SLAVERY To The BISHOPRIC

In The A. M. E. Church

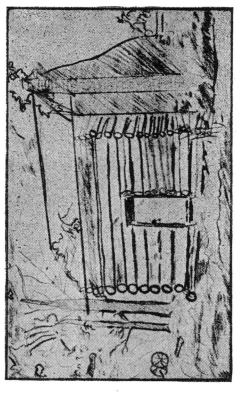

The Log Hut in Elbert County, Ga., on the plantation of Thomas Jones, where Bishop Heard was born. June 25, 1850,

FROM
SLAVERY To The BISHOPRIC

In The A. M. E. Church

An Autobiography

BY

WILLIAM H. HEARD, D.D., LL.D.

One of the Bishops of the

A. M. E. Church

1924

THE A. M. E. BOOK CONCERN
D. M. BAXTER, Manager
631 Pine Street   Philadelphia, Pa.
Publishers

CONTENTS

ILLUSTRATIONS

DEDICATION

I sacredly and solemnly dedicate this little book to the self-made men in the ministry of the African Methodist Episcopal Church, who have, and are giving their lives to the Sacred Cause of preaching the Gospel and advancing the Church.

W. H. HEARD.

INTRODUCTION

*"Heights by great men reached
        and kept
    Were not attained by sudden
        flight,
But they, while their companions
        slept,
    Were toiling upward in the
        night."*

                    —Longfellow.

Every man in this life has a part to
play, and, leaves a footprint, seen and
followed by—some other. How well
that part is played depends very largely
on the man. It may be played loosely—
carelessly—without a thought of anything but the NOW, the present; without any thought of its scope in reaching, touching, or influencing another's
life. It is a footprint, nevertheless,

and some one follows in it and is
stunted in life, perhaps for life.

On the other hand that part may be
played with great care as to every de-
tail, with much toil in preparation,
with the thought ever in view that "no
man lives to himself alone," but that
we are building character and making
men, how careful, then must one be in
the CHOICE and USE of the material
that tends to the "making" men.

With the idea in view that "He that
believeth shall not make haste" such a
one is mindful to be diligent. "Whatso-
ever his hands find to do, to do that
with all his power," patiently, firmly,
believing that "The race is not to the
swift, but to him that endureth to the
end"—such a man is blessed in his
doing, gaining knowledge, and experi-
ence from the every-day things that
confront him, and which he masters.
He, therefore, solves the problem of
real living, learns the lesson of true

success, and thus plants such footprints on "the sands of time" that observing ones are impressed thereby, and encouraged to follow them, seeing they lead to service and to honor.

It is highly fitting, then, that we should have before our youth in particular, and ourselves in general, the histories and biographies of men who have risen from the depths of ordinary life, beset with hardship, prejudice, and ostracism, and in spite of all this, with perseverance and strong determination, have risen to the heights in the various positions in the affairs of this life; and that we may note the HOW they have risen, and the WHY they have attained these goals. These incentives can only be had in the spoken or written narration of this progression.

Hence it is timely that those who have so attained should pause sufficently long to give a published sketch of their lives—a footprint—that those seeing and reading may be inspired to take hope, to labor, and press on to the goal with the object in view of rendering the greatest and best service to mankind in general.

Such a character is shown, and such a service has been, and is being rendered by the author of this little book, a man who has kept in touch with men in all the walks of life, no matter how lowly or degraded, or how exalted in station, yet ever with a kind word of encouragement, an eye of sympathy, and a stretched-out hand to help and to lift up.

So, after many importunities and requests by men in the various ranks of life, who have listened to the eloquence of, and noticed the untiring, yet effective labors of this earnest servant of Christ, and for human uplift, Bishop William H. Heard has yielded, and consented to give a brief sketch of his life—a compressed autobiography—in which we may note his career from the "slave pen" (twice sold as human chattel), to a representative of this, the greatest government on earth, as United States Minister Resident and Consul General to Liberia, Africa— and how from an humble "Cornfield Exhorter" in the State of Georgia to a General Officer, and now a Bishop in (to my mind), the greatest Church on earth, presiding over the First and historic district of the African Methodist Episcopal Church.

Such an autobiography can but inspire our Race, and in a time when others would discredit, and say we "have failed in spite of education and religious opportunities, and have not made good"—it is with pride that we may deny the false statements, and point to such lives, and to such a character of progress as the author of this book: "From Slavery to the Bishopric in the A. M. E. Church."

H. H. COOPER, Ph. D.,
Director of A. M. E. Church Survey,
First Episcopal District, Philadelphia,
  Penna.

Bishop W. H. Heard, D.D., LL.D.,
January, 1924.

FOREWORD

Those who may read this little booklet, *The Autobiography of my life*, I hope may be benefitted and encouraged, especially the young men and women of our Race.

They can see that men make progress without opportunity, and they ought to be encouraged to use the opportunities they have to make greater progress.

Opportunity comes but once, if properly used it is a great asset, if neglected the person is the poorer for having neglected it.

"It is bald-headed behind,
   When passed, cannot be grasped,
Therefore seize it in the front,
   And use it before it passes."

This booklet is written at the request of many friends. I have no desire to parade who I am and what I am,

because my defects will do that; but I
do desire to help the young people of a
race so deprived of educational and
material opportunities. While they are
ten times, yea, one hundred times
better today than in the past, yet they
are not equal to other people's. My
defects are so glaring that I feel almost
ashamed to put my thoughts in print;
but so much depends upon those who
have courage, whether they have education or not, that I am encouraged to
pen these lines.

The autobiography, itself will show
the depth from which the subject came
and the height he has aimed at and
attained.

A minister of the Gospel is an am-
bassador of the Lord, and a commis-
sioner of the High Court of Heaven.
If he can faintly proclaim the message
given, he performs a great duty.

To be a Bishop in the African Methodist Episcopal Church is a privilege,

if properly used, that few have, so the Bishop ought to be a man of life, and a father in Israel. He should so conduct himself that men will be impressed by his writings and by his words. Therefore, as a Bishop, I am sending forth these words of a life lived in the midst of privation, ignorance, and slavery, hoping that they may be a means in this enlightened day, of helping those who have a better opportunity and who are encouraged to use those opportunities.

The A. M. E. Church is an instrument in this country that has done, and is doing more for the uplift of the Race than any instrument conditioned as it is; I, therefore write this booklet as an A. M. E. Bishop, using the A. M. E. Church as a vehicle to carry it to the ends of the earth.

May it be the means of extending my life while I live, and continuing it when I am dead.

CHAPTER ONE
BIRTH

William Henry (Harrison) Heard was born in Elbert County, Georgia, ten miles below Elberton Court House, and three miles from Longstreet, a small town with one store and Post Office.

He was born in a log cabin. The logs were cut promiscuously from small pines, straight and crooked, and they were built like a stable or a pen of any kind. Where a log was too crooked, or left too large a hole, it was "chipped out" so as to be made to lay closer together, in the same way they built a pig pen or horse stable. The only difference, where they built a house for living was, they took the bark off the trees and chinked the cracks in winter and knocked out the chinking in summer.

In October they would chink and daub so as to make the house warm, and in May they would knock out the chinking so as to make the house cool.

During this season of the year frogs, lizards, snakes, and smaller insects would play "hide and seek" out of one crack into the other. At night you would just as liable find a snake curled up in your bed taking his rest as you were to go and take your rest.

The chimneys were built of pine sticks daubed with mud about four to five feet high, they were as good an entrance and exit as the door. The house had one door about three feet by five feet, one window about two feet by three feet, the floor was made of "puncheons," that is: the slabs were sawed off the trees intended for sawing planks. You could count the chickens under these houses as accurately through these cracks as you could in the yard.

I was born June 25, 1850. This they called at that time "Corn plowing time." So when they designated my age, they would say: "He was born in corn plowing time, in, or about the year when the stars fell," or some incident of note.

A woman who had children regularly was called a "breeder" in those days; and was allowed to go home at ten o'clock in the morning each day, again at twelve, and at three to nurse the child; for the child was reckoned as "property," and therefore valuable enough to be given this time.

My mother was a farm hand, and was considered a "breeder," so that in plowing time she worked right around her house, and plowed with an old horse by the name of "Selim." She never went away with the rest of the hands, two and three miles from the house. Not my mother only, but all women who were nursing children,

were thus dealt with.   The attention
to the babies was given by the larger
children, who looked after the smaller
ones.

My father lived three miles away.
He would come in on Wednesday
nights after things had closed up at his
home, and be back at his home by daylight Thursday mornings; come again
Saturday night, and return by daylight
Monday morning.   He had a pass
weekly from his master that gave him
this permission.

The night my mother died (I was
nine years of age), I lay on a pallet
next to a cradle and rocked my infant
brother who was just five weeks old,
and gave him the bottle all night.   I did
this when only nine years of age myself.

CHAPTER TWO

FIRST AND SECOND TIMES SOLD

My father, George W. Heard, was a slave of Thomas Heard, who was reputed to be his father. He was a blacksmith by trade, and while he weighed only one hundred and forty pounds, he could use a sledge hammer as steadily and actively as a man weighing two hundred pounds, and shoe as many mules as any blacksmith in the county.

After thirty years as a blacksmith, he took up the trades of a wheelwright and a carpenter, and worked at all three of these trades twenty years before he died.

He did not know figures at all, yet he could give a bill for lumber as accurately as a master mathematician.

He never belonged to the same man that my mother belonged to, but lived

near enough to see her once or twice a
week.

My mother was Pathenia Galloway;
she and her children belonged to the
Galloway estate (two boys: Wylie and
George Galloway).

When the boys became of age and the
estate was settled, my mother and her
three children were placed upon the
auction block and sold to the highest
bidder. That man was Lindsay Smith,
who lived at Rock Fence, in the flat-
woods of Elbert County. He was a
large farmer, and owned nearly one
hundred Negroes. This was my first
time sold.

After two or three years at Rock
Fence a man by the name of John A.
Trenchard, principal of the high school
at Elberton, Georgia, wanted to buy a
cook. He came to Lindsay Smith, who
had a woman by the name of Harriet
and her children to sell, but Prof.
Trenchard saw us children, and asked

MRS. PARTHENIA JONES (the mother of Bishop Heard) plowing "Old Selim" on the plantation of Thomas Jones, in Elbert Co., Ga., 1850.

for the woman who was the mother of these children, and was shown my mother. There were then four children, as Cordelia, my youngest sister, was born, but the difference in the sale was one thousand dollars more. He paid the difference and purchased my mother and her four children—Millie, Henry, Beverly, and Delia. We went to Elberton, my mother became the cook and two of us, large enough to do errands, became house servants; as Prof. Trenchard kept a boarding house and many of the students boarded with him.

This was my second and last time to be sold as a slave.

Prof. Trenchard was an Iowa man, and what we considered a fair master; but there were many men in Georgia very cruel as masters, for the law did not interfere with a master and his slave. It had nothing to do with his treatment of them, and there was no law in vogue as to cruelty to animals in those days.

I knew a man living just three miles from us who beat a woman belonging to him to death, and she was heavily pregnant; so he was guilty of the murder of two, instead of one person.

Many of the masters had cruel overseers and Negro drivers, who were allowed to beat the Negroes, but not to take life.

Many men and women resented this cruelty, and would fight back, but the overseers would overpower them, and the master would stand by and see this overseer or driver put one hundred lashes on their bare backs and wash them down with salt and water. The blood would run from their heads to their heels; yet many of them were never conquered. They would go to the woods and stay there months, yes, some of them years. They would dig caves in the ground and live in them.

So they would get the Negro hounds to trail them and catch them; but many of them would take a scythe and cut these hounds into pieces as they approached.

Others had "remedies" that they used that the hounds could not scent them, so they could not be trailed; for they could be within five feet of the hounds and they could not scent them.

I knew a woman who could not be conquered by her mistress, and so her master threatened to sell her to New Orleans Negro traders. She took her right hand, laid it down on a meat block and cut off three fingers, and thus made the sale impossible; but I will not recount these cruelties further.

After living at Elberton Court House two years, my mother became the mother of her last child, George Clark.

Typhoid fever broke out as an epidemic. My oldest sister and my mother died in this epidemic. Myself, Beverly, Cordelia, and George Clark were left orphans. I was nine years of age, the oldest of the four. George Clark, the youngest, was just five weeks old. This was about the year 1859.

When I became ten years of age I began working on the farm. A plow was made just to suit my height, and I plowed day after day. So we went on until 1865.

One day in 1865 I was plowing with a mare called "Old Jane," and I looked and saw the "Yankees." I had heard before of their coming. I took out Old Jane and went to the house about three o'clock in the afternoon. I was asked why I had come home at that hour. I told them "I was afraid the Yankees would steal my horse, so I brought her home," but that was not the cause at all. Freedom had come, and I came to meet it.

Four weeks after that I was stacking hay one day, and the "boss man" came out where we were at work. He was under the influence of drink and he beat everybody. That night I took all my belongings, put them in a pocket handkerchief and "went to freedom." Thus ended slavery with me.

CHAPTER THREE

MY EDUCATION

I attended Sunday School when I was ten years of age, in Elberton, Georgia, at the Methodist Episcopal Church South. We did not learn to read nor to write, as it was against the law for any person to teach any slave to read; and any slave caught writing suffered the penalty of having his fore-finger cut from his right hand; yet there were some who could read and write.

In this Sunday School we were taught the Bible and the Catechism, and committed much to memory by having the same repeated to us in the Sunday School, and then some member of the white family carried this out during the week; so that there were those of us who could repeat whole Psalms and chapter after chapter in the Shorter Catechism.

This was the education that came to a slave, and I for one had five years of this kind of training.

At the end of five years freedom came; but there were no teachers in the part of the county in which I lived and no schools for Negroes.

My father was a wheelwright and had a shop on the main road, not far from the town school, so I secured the services of a "poor white" boy named Billee Adams and paid him ten cents a lesson and studied in Webster's Blue Back Spelling Book. I studied spelling, reading, and arithmetic all in this one book.

After six months the year 1865 ended and I was hired to a farmer by the name of William Henry Heard, from whom I received my name. The contract was five dollars per month and a recitation each night. I worked from "kin to cant," that is: from daylight to dark. When I came in, put up my mule, and fed him, I made my way to the dining room and waited for my teacher to finish his supper, then I recited my lesson to him. I had added another study, writing, to my curriculum, and my hour for study was twelve o'clock in the day. We were given one hour for dinner and feeding our stock. Many of the hands slept this hour. I spent it in the preparation of my lessons for the night.

Boys had no pockets in their clothes in those days, so I cut the board back from my book and carried it on my head, under my cap. It was safe unless a hard rain came up, then cap, book, and all suffered.

After we laid by the crops in June, I went to Elberton Court House and **attended school** six weeks under a **young man named** George H. Washington, from Augusta, Georgia. I studied spelling, reading, writing, arithmetic, and geography. At the end of this time I could spell words of five or six syllables, compose, and write a letter and understood the four rules of arithmetic: addition, subtraction, multiplication, and division. This was only a Summer school, and we all returned to the farm at the end of six weeks.

I kept up my studies with a farmer until Christmas. At Christmas I was hired to another farmer by the name of Clay Hulmes. He had attended the High School and was prepared to give me a great deal of help, but he was a "poor boy" and much prejudiced, but our contract was six dollars per month, board, and a lesson at night.

While I had three or four studies he would only have me recite one study each night. After six months I left him. I had broken the contract and my father felt bound to make me carry it out, so he sent me back. I stayed three days and broke it again, so they all decided that it was best that we stay apart.

By this time we had a regular school in the town taught by a lady by the name of Mrs. Hankinson. I worked at my father's shop morning and evening, and attended this school for six weeks, which so prepared me that in the Fall I began teaching school myself, and with a private teacher I carried forward my studies and was able to stand an examination and teach the three months public school, which was a great help to me financially, for we were allowed one dollar per month per scholar, and with an assistant I had one hundred or more pupils, so that I had at the close of this school term over three hundred dollars in money, and that was big money in those days, and it gave me a start in the world of economics. During this teaching I took lessons from a white man by the name of James Lofton. I studied grammar, mathematics, and history. When I learned the parts of speech in Smith's Grammar and their relation to each other, it was a revellation to me. I saw opening up along the intellectual horizon things I never dreamed of. I was a man of good memory, they said, and I got much from my studies, so that I went on teaching and in the second year I received a second grade certificate, taught the Public School and was rewarded as before.

In January, 1873, I went to Mt. Carmel, South Carolina, where I had a six months public school and a regular salary of forty dollars per month. I taught here four years and continued my studies under the township school teacher of the white school, a Mrs. Ritchie, who taught me algebra and Latin.

The State of South Carolina at that time was Republican and the University of South Carolina at that time was under State control, as it is now. There were scholarships in each county, and any boy over sixteen years of age and under twenty-one years could compete for these scholarships. Abbeyville County, in which I lived, was entitled to five. I won one of these scholarships, entered the University and received twenty dollars per month. With that I supported my family and myself. I entered as a freshman, but in 1877, when the Democrats came in power, they turned out all the Colored students. I was a sophomore in the classical department at the time.

Being a member of the Legislature from Abbeyville County, I was unseated by the Democrats and refused a school in the county because of my interest in politics.

I returned to Georgia and opened a school in the African Methodist Episcopal Church at Athens. At the end

of the Summer School, for that was all
that we had, I entered Clarke University, spent one term there and then
was persuaded to enter Atlanta University. I spent one year as a Junior
in the classical department. At the
end of this year I had a governmental
position and so I left school until I
came to Philadelphia in August, 1888.
I then entered the Reformed Episcopal
Seminary at Forty-first and Chestnut
Streets, Philadelphia, studied Theol-
ogy, Hebrew, and Greek, and took the
Extension Course of Lectures at the
University of Pennsylvania. Thus
ended the patchwork of such an education as I have been able to pick up.

I have Honorary Degree of Doctor
of Divinity (D. D.) from Allen University, also from Wilberforce University; Doctor of Laws (LL. D.) from
Campbell College, Jackson, Mississippi.
These titles are honorary; given to me
because of the position I occupy in the
Church more than from learning.

CHAPTER FOUR

IN POLITICS

At the close of the war I was but fifteen years of age, and yet I had much to do with the politics of the county in which I lived (Elbert County).

Colonel James T. Ackerman, who was the United States Attorney General under President Ulysses S. Grant, and who lived in that county, was a staunch Republican and encouraged me much along this line. In 1872 I had just reached my majority and was the County Chairman of the Republican Party, and looked after the interests of that party together with a man by the name of Nathan Thompson, who could neither read nor write. Our tickets for the election of 1872 were printed, and distributed by the State Chairman. While our Postmaster was a Republican, yet by some Democratic move our tickets were intercepted and were not allowed to reach us. We had no railroad and got mail only every other day, so that when the mail came in on Monday, or the day before the election, no tickets came in it. So in order to have tickets the next day at the polls, I wrote tickets all night, and five hundred tickets were cast at that precinct. Had we received our tickets and distributed them at each precinct the county would have gone Republican, but as it was we lost the county.

I was a condidate for the Legislature on the Republican ticket, Grant and Colfax were the candidates for President and Vice-President.

In 1876 I was in South Carolina. It was called "THE RED-SHIRT CAMPAIGN," and will never be forgotten for its bloody deeds. Yet the Republicans stood their ground and won out in many counties. I was a candidate

for the Legislature on the Republican
ticket, from Abbeyville County. We
carried the county by over one thousand majority. I carried my precinct,
Calhoun Mills, by three hundred and
fifteen.

On the night before the election we
gathered all the Republican voters
together in a school-house near the
precinct, sang and prayed, drank coffee
and ate sandwiches all night.

Just at daylight we marched to the
polls and stood in line until we had
voted five hundred Republican votes. I
was Deputy United States Marshal
and had the conflict of my life, but we
were three to one. Every man armed
with some kind of a weapon and each
stood by his post. We counted our
votes and left the polls about three
o'clock in the morning when the Democrats undertook to capture our re-
turns; but we were too strong for

them; however, they did capture them after we had left.

On Saturday I returned to the precinct to get affidavits from the managers of the election. I was captured by the Democrats, my hands tied behind me, and carried into Elbert County, where they made a fire in an old school-house. We remained there all night. I was tied to two of these men, so if they fell asleep I could not get away.

The next morning I was carried to Ruckersville, where they all drank whisky. The South Carolina mob tried to get these Georgians to do away with me; but they did not have the courage, or they were too proud of me as a Georgian to do so.

At the fall of night they carried me to Ed Starke's, with whom I had had trouble on election day in 1872, and tried to get him to do their deed, but his father said: "There can be no killing on my place." So after supper, about eight o'clock at night, they took me down to Broad River, had a Colored man to put me across and released me.

I was thirty miles from the railroad, in Wilkes County, but, I knew my territory so that I walked that thirty miles and was at Washington-Wilkes the next morning at daylight.

I hid around until the train blew, then I went aboard and lay down as a sick man. When the conductor came around for tickets I played off that I was too sick to have bought a ticket. I had five dollars in my pockets and I paid my way to Augusta, Georgia, went across the river to Hamburg, South Carolina, and stated to the captain of the troops stationed there who I was and what position I held. He sent me to Columbia, where I made an affidavit of the vote of my precinct, which gave the State to Hayes and Wheeler, as we had a Republican majority of three hundred and fifteen. I took my seat as a member of the Legislature from Abbeyville County, and sat during that session; but at the end of the session the Democrats contested our seats and unseated us. The troops were removed and the State turned over to the Democrats.

In 1880 I was appointed railway postal clerk by the direction of Congressman Emory Speare, an independent Democrat, for whom I had canvassed, and whose election I had helped to secure. I (in my route) ran from Lula to Athens, Georgia, from Atlanta, to Macon, Georgia, and from Atlanta, Georgia, to Charlotte, North Carolina, for two years. I resigned this position to enter the ministry. After this I took no great interest in politics until February, 1895, when by the assistance of Bishop Henry McNeil Turner, I was appointed by President Grover Cleveland United States Minister Resident and Consul General to Liberia, West Coast Africa, which position I held for four years.

At the same time I preached regularly and built the church at Monrovia, Liberia, from the funds received from the government, and not from the Church.

The Eliza Turner Memorial Chapel stands there today as a crowning effort and a token of my interest in the Church.

CHAPTER FIVE

TRAVEL

Travel with me became a great charm and fact. I had not left the State in which I was born until I was twenty-three years of age. I then went to South Carolina, where I taught school, and remained within the bounds of this State for four years.

After that I returned to Georgia and taught school four years more without leaving the State;; but in 1883 I was appointed to Aiken, South Carolina, and remained there two years.

At the end of two years I went to Charleston, South Carolina, and after the earthquake in 1886, the damage done to my church compelled me to go North. I visited Philadelphia, Baltimore, New York and Boston. This opened up a new world to me. During that summer I went to Wilberforce, Ohio, and saw my Church and Race as I had not seen it before.

In 1888 I came to Philadelphia to live and have remained here up to the present day, yet I served Wilmington, Delaware, and Harrisburg, Pennsylvania. I was appointed from Harrisburg United States Minister to Liberia, February, 1895.

This gave me an opportunity to cross the ocean. I had dreaded all my life this great body of water, and I entered upon its bosom with much timidity. I took the "Norramandie" steamship for Southampton in March, 1895, and arrived at Southampton at midnight, eight days after, took the train to London, arriving there at two o'clock in the morning, and drove to the Hotel Finsbury, on Finsbury Pavement. I was soon directed to my room, where I spent a few hours.

Arising early I visited London with a guide. I went to St. Paul's Cathedral, the greatest Church in the world. I also visited Westminster Abbey and looked upon the graves of poets, statesmen and crowned heads; here the Wesleys, Livingstone and Stanley are deposited.

I visited the Parliament, the great Congress House of England, and the British Museum, which, perhaps, has no equal for antiquity in the world. The Pharoahs and Rameses are here to be seen, and no one can mistake them for Caucasian; they are African. These mummies are the exact likenesses of those old kings and show that they belong to the Hamitic race.

The oldest copies of the "Book of Books" (The Bible) are to be seen here. This Museum requires more than a week's survey in order to be able to tell what is there. I did not stay that long at this time, but I had a week, and more than a week, at another time. Any traveler going East seeking information will find it here.

I visited the "Crystal Palace," a building of pure crystal, covering an acre of land; I have never seen its equal. The exhibition that is shown here, day after day, and year after year, is not only informing, but thrilling.

Finding that Bishop H. M. Turner was in Liverpool on his way to Africa, I cut my stay short and joined him at Liverpool.

An incident occurred to me as I was leaving London that will occur to any stranger, that is: when I went to settle my bill I asked the clerk how much it was. While I knew shillings and pounds, her expression confused me. I said, "What is my bill?" She said: "Eleven and six." I did not know what eleven and six was, so I gave her two sovereigns, and asked her if she could get it out of them. She informed me that she could get it out of one of them. I learned afterwards that the bill was eleven and one-half shillings, and that there are twenty shillings in a pound or sovereign. I had eight and one-half shillings change from one sovereign. But I was yet confused, for I had had a draft cashed that morning and part of it was in gold and part in paper.

The English five-pound notes look like tissue paper. I paid no attention to the notes at all, and mistook them to be paper to wrap my gold coin in. But finding that I was seventy-five dollars short, I looked on this "tissue paper" and found that it had printing on it, so I took it to the cashier and asked her if it would explain anything concerning the fifteen pounds I was short. She informed me that each of these three pieces of tissue paper was a five-pound note, making fifteen pounds in all, the amount of my supposed fifteen pounds shortage. I rejoiced at my discovery and went away a wiser man.

I reached Liverpool early in the morning and sought a restaurant for my breakfast. But restaurants in the East do not open until ten o'clock in the morning, and, therefore, do not serve breakfast, so I sought the railroad people and was able to get breakfast. I then went to the landing and found Bishop Turner ready to sail on the "Calabar."

At ten o'clock we weighed anchor and started for the west coast of Africa. But learning that a storm was raging outside of the bar we anchored and remained all night. Sunday morning we continued our journey.

After six days we were in the Bay of Biscay, called the "Ocean Graveyard."

It was very rough and Bishop Turner was very much afraid. The boat was a cargo boat and the front was very low, so we shipped thousands of tons of water.

Bishop Turner became very much excited and said: "Heard this ship is liable to sink at any minute." He went on the bridge and asked the captain. The captain told him yes, it was liable to sink at any minute. He came back and informed me of the condition. I went to my room and went to bed. He remained on deck tramping water knee deep part of the time.

A school of flying fish flew into our boat and the seamen said: "This is a bad omen." That did not help us any, but increased our excitement. About ten o'clock at night the storm seemed to have reached its height. Bishop Turner came to my room and said: "Heard, how can you lie down here and sleep. It looks like the boat will go down any minute." I told him I could not help the case, therefore I had gotten where I could not see what was going on.

Next morning the storm had subsided. We had about crossed the Bay and were nearing the Canary Islands.

Sunday morning at sunrise we were all on deck sighting the Canary Islands. At ten o'clock in the morning we were anchored off Las Palmas, the principal city of Grand Canary Island. We went ashore and attended services at the Church of England, where we heard a sermon preached in English. It was an Easter sermon, as this was Easter Sunday.

After the sermon we went to the hotel and had our dinner. Very little English was spoken anywhere on the island, but we had gotten along well up to this time, because we had a guide.

After dinner Bishop Turner said: "I will go back on the boat and spend the night." I told him I would remain off all night. But after he was gone and the guide had left me all the English was gone.

I found it impossible to make myself understood, so I could not remain all night. I went out, got a taxi and returned to the boat, where I remained all night.

The next day was Easter Monday, a holiday, so that everything was quiet, the ship getting supplies as best she could. In the afternoon we sailed for Sierra Leone, and reached there the following Sunday.

As we reached this African town of forty thousand inhabitants and less than one-fourth of them civilized, we felt good, for here we met our people. Up to this time we had been with the

other race, which was not very custom-
ary to us.

We "American Daddies" were wel-
comed by the natives. They followed
us by the hundreds and rejoiced at our
coming.

The Annual Conference met imme-
diately with five or six native preachers and three Americans. It was a
great conference, and much interest
was manifested in our coming, and in
our work.

The Governor of the Colony, Colonel
Cardew, gave a dinner, and invited the
Bishop, the United States Minister and
Presiding Elders, Steady and Frederick. This showed appreciation of the
work we were trying to do in the Colony.

After a few days we were on our
way to Liberia, two hundred and forty
miles south, and landed in twenty-six
hours. As we touched the soil of this

little Republic, a thrill of joy and gratitude went through us. There the American emigrant met us in large numbers.

We had no African Methodist Episcopal Church, so we held the Conference in the Methodist Episcopal Church through the courtesy of the pastor.

Being the United States Minister and reaching there officially, I so informed the Government that I had come to reside as Minister Resident and Consul General of the United States, and had my letter of credence, which I desired to present. I was informed that Thursday at twelve o'clock, noon, would be fixed as the day and hour for my reception and its reception.

On that day and at that hour, Bishop Turner and myself were at the Executive Mansion. There we met the President and Cabinet, who received us.

The Government is modeled after our

(the U. S.) Government.   The President, Hon. J. J. Cheeseman, of Georgia, an emigrant from that State; Vice President, Hon. J. J. Ross, an emigrant from Georgia; Secretary of State, Hon. G. W. Gibson, an emigrant from Baltimore, Maryland; Secretary of the Treasury, Hon. Arthur Barclay, a West Indian; Attorney General, Hon. F. E. R. Johnson, a Liberian; Secretary of Education, Hon. S. J. Dennis, a Liberian;; Secretary of the Interior, Hon. J. H. Moore, an emigrant from South Carolina; Secretary of War and Navy, Hon. A. D. Williams, an emigrant from Virginia. These men made up the Cabinet of this Republic.   It is not a wonder that they have done so little; but it is a wonder that they have done so much.

We delivered our Letter of Credence, made our address of friendship, followed by Bishop Turner, and was responded to by the President himself and the Secretary of State, after which a banquet was served in real American style for all the representatives of the different governments, who drank toasts to the Liberian and American Governments.

In 1896 we returned to America and visited the General Conference at Wilmington, North Carolina, being a delegate from the Liberia Conference.

After sixty days leave, we returned to Liberia in company of Mrs. Heard as far as England, and made our first visit to France.

This country is the highest in its recognition of man without regard to color of any I have ever visited. The art of painting, drawing and sculpture gives every visitor an opportunity to learn and be inspired as he visits "The Louvre." The hotels are first-class, and every person gets first-class accommodation if he can pay for it.

From Paris we went to Genoa, Florence, Milan, Bologne, Venice and Geneva. It is not our purpose in this little book to describe these cities, but one visiting them will come home wiser and better from what he sees, and the contact with these people. We also visited the World's Sunday School Convention at Zurich, Switzerland, and found these people devoid of prejudice. Prejudice across the Channel among the Latin races is not so apparent as on this side the Channel among the English-speaking people. America puts her virus into these people from New York weekly, and they seem to be easily inoculated, so that in certain parts of London and Liverpool the prejudice is as great as in New York.

My American travel was while I was serving four years, without salary, and without traveling expenses as Secretary-treasurer of the Connectional Preachers' Aid and Mutual Relief Association. I traveled in every State in the Union, except Maine, New Hampshire, Vermont and North Dakota. I attended every Annual Conference in the A. M. E. Church. Yearly I spent four months on the road, two and three nights in a week curled up on a bench in a "jim crow" car. I never used a pass, but paid for every trip during those four years without any funds from the Church treasury.

This travel has been the greatest school to me, and a school in which any person may invest; for in the United States and in the different States you will get lessons that you do not get at your home or in some other State.

In the countries abroad a man obtains from contact what he can never obtain from books. My travel in Africa gave me knowledge that I would not exchange for that I have obtained from the books I have read concerning that country.

My contact with the people of England, France, Germany, Italy and Switzerland also gave me knowledge of those countries and of those people that made me know them better than I could have known them by reading history.

My advice to young people is to travel. If you have little, sacrifice and travel to the extent of what you have, and travel with your eyes and your mind open. If you have much, go abroad and take time and spend a month in Paris, a month in Germany, a month in Rome, and a month in London, as I have done. It will pay if you expect a future.

CHAPTER SIX

MY CONVERSION

The word "Conversion" is used inter-changeably with "Regeneration." Many of us use this word without thinking of the depth to which the meaning takes us.

I was nine years at the altar, every year seeking CONVERSION. I had been told by many ministers during these nine years that all I had to do was to believe on the Lord. This word, BE-LIEVE, to me meant only to accredit things; but when I sought the Lord I accredited Him as the Omnipotent, Omnipresent, and Omniscient God; but I could not conceive that He was MY FATHER, and, therefore, the rela-tionship of a father was to be had by FAITH. So I had sought the Lord all

these years without faith in Him as a
Father, and myself as His child. But
year after year I became more and
more confident that He loved me, that
He gave His Son to die for me, and that
the NEW BIRTH fully established this
relation, and that when I could reach
that New Birth by faith in Christ as
The Redeemer of the world, and of
man in particular, that my relation as
Son was not only established, but rejoiced in; so that at a protracted meeting in Athens, Georgia, April and May,
1879, I attended the meeting and was at
the altar every night for five weeks.

One night before the services began,
I reached the conclusion that open confession of my sins and acknowledgement of Christ as My Savior was the
thing to do. But I lacked faith to do
this, because I had felt nothing to as-
sure me that I was saved. So I carried
out the idea by getting up in my seat

and undertaking to make this confession and acknowledgement.

After some time standing on my feet, being unable to speak, FAITH CAME, my mouth flew open and I shouted for joy, and then I openly acknowledged that I was a sinner and that Christ was my Savior, and that I was willing and ready to surrender ALL to Him.

When I did this the burden of guilt left me, and I felt that I was forgiven and the only thing I had to do was to live in fellowship with Him. And this I have tried to do all these years. Therefore I believe that I have turned my face in the right direction, and am walking in the direction prescribed in the Scriptures. And, so long as I walk therein, I am converted, or regenerated, a Son of God, a Brother of Christ, and an Heir of Heaven.

CHAPTER SEVEN

THE MINISTRY

Exhorter.

On May 16, 1879, I was converted. At that time I was teaching school and living with Colonel W. A. Pledger, at Athens, Georgia. He was a lawyer and I felt that to be my calling; so I had been reading Blackstone in preparation to be admitted to the bar, and to make law my profession. But, after my conversion, I felt the call to the ministry, and was so impressed that when the Quarterly Conference met in June, 1879, I applied for license to exhort, as that is the first step for a preacher in the Methodist Church.

The Rev. Peter McClain was the Presiding Elder. He was a man without literary training, yet he could read,

write and preach a good gospel sermon.
I had gone before my class and they
had sent me to the Quarterly Conference.   I was prepared educationally to
stand the examination, but in those
days many questions were asked to find
out if the applicant had gifts, graces,
and really had been called to the ministry.

I exhorted for three months. I did
not preach, but exhorted; for an exhorter was not permitted to take a text,
but he read a chapter, or part of a chapter and proceeded to explain the same
as he understood it.

Local Preacher

At the end of three months I had
gone before the Church, preached a
trial sermon, and they had recommended me to be licensed as a local
preacher.

My trial sermon lasted about six minutes. I had said all I knew, and I sat down. I have kept that up these forty years, that when I get through to sit down.

While I only spoke six minutes, the Church was impressed that I had been called to the ministry, so after an examination by the Quarterly Conference it recommended me for local preacher's license. I taught Sunday School, led a class, and preached whenever called upon for three months.

Traveling Licentiate

At the end of these three months the Quarterly Conference recommended me, and I made application to join the Annual Conference. I joined the North Georgia Annual Conference at Macon, Georgia, under Bishop Jabez Pitt Campbell, January 12, 1880.

I was examined for admission by the Revs. Andrew Brown, Robert Anderson, W. P. Graham, L. Thomas, J. W. Randolph and E. P. Holmes, and on the 12th day of January the committee reported, and I, with Revs. P. B. Peters, A. L. Shaw, William Upshur, L. G. Gary, Jordan R. Gay and others were admitted to the North Georgia Annual Conference.

At that time there were only two conferences in the State of Georgia, and in February (1880) Bishop Joseph Simeon Flipper was admitted to the other conference (the Georgia Annual Conference), so that in January, 1924, I shall have traveled in the itineracy for forty-four years, and in February Bishop Flipper shall have traveled the same length of time.

When the Conference adjourned and the appointments were read, I was read out for Johntown; no members, no church, only the name of the place. But at the end of the year I reported a church with eleven members, and Conference Claims for every department. The Church was paid for. I had purchased a school house for a church.

I carried to the Annual Conference twenty-five dollars for personal expenses. In those days we were building schools, and when the roll was called the Presiding Elders and Pastors of large churches were asked to pay five dollars, and all ministers one dollar. But I paid my first five dollars on Morris Brown College the year that I was admitted, and have never paid less at any conference I attended, and have never carried less than twenty-five dollars for personal expenses to an Annual Conference since 1880.

Deacon

In 1881 the Annual Conference met at Atlanta, Georgia. I was examined in the first year and second year studies and ordained a Deacon by Bishop William Fisher Dickerson. I had served my first year at Johntown Mission, and at the adjournment of this conference was returned for the second year. In 1882, when the conference met, I reported Johntown Mission with fifty-three members, and it was a Circuit instead of a Mission.

Elder

When the appointments were read, I was read out for Markham Street Mission, Atlanta, Georgia. I only served this point a few months and was transferred to Aiken, South Carolina. But before being transferred, I passed the Fourth Year Class and Bishop Dickerson ordained me an Elder at Washington, Georgia. Bishop Wesley John Gaines was chairman of the committee that examined me.

I served Aiken ten months, built a

parsonage, renovated the Church, took in one hundred and sixty members at a revival, and reported the church out of debt.

Conference met this year at Georgetown, South Carolina, and I was appointed to Marion, South Carolina, but the Church at Aiken telegraphed the Bishop not to send any one else, so, in three days I was back to Aiken for the second year. We had great success, and at the conference held at Beaufort, South Carolina, I was appointed to Mt. Zion Church, Charleston, South Carolina.

When I came to Aiken, it only paid three hundred and fifty-five dollars a year, yet I resigned a government position paying me eleven hundred and fifty dollars a year. This station paid me the first year six hundred and fifty dollars; the second year, six hundred and eighty dollars, two suits

of clothes each year and perquisites
that amounted to two or three hundred
dollars. But coming to Mt. Zion I had
an appointment that would pay me one
thousand dollars, house rent, fuel, and
perquisites amounting to four or five
hundred dollars, which took me above
the salary I was receiving when I left
the railway mail service.

This church was in debt to the
amount of ten thousand, three hundred
and fifty dollars, besides, they owed a
current debt of more than fifteen hundred dollars. But in the course of six
months I had met all the obligations
and had gotten down to the bonded
debt. I remained here three years,
and at no time could my regular con-
gregation be seated without bringing in
chairs. I paid the bonded debt down
to five thousand dollars, put in a pipe
organ for two thousand and five hundred dollars, and renovated the church

after the earthquake at a cost of one thousand and eight hundred dollars. All of this was paid when I left by transfer for the Philadelphia Annual Conference. During these three years I received eleven hundred persons in the church.

Transferring from Bishop B. W. Arnett to Bishop H. M. Turner, I was appointed to Allen Chapel, Philadelphia, an appointment Bishop Levi Jenkins Coppin had held until he was elected editor of the A. M. E. Church Review. We had one of the greatest revivals that had taken place in the city of Philadelphia for many years. This revival ran for four weeks, and we took into our church alone one hundred and thirty-one persons, who I put into a class and led them with the assistance of a lady named Martha Morris, who proved to be a great leader, so that when these persons were ready for full member-

ship, we lost not more than eight or
ten out of a class of one hundred and
thirty-one.

This, perhaps, was the greatest num-
ber ever received at any one time in Allen Chapel.   Allen Chapel since that
time has grown to be "Allen Church."
We only remained there one year, and
by our own choice we were moved and
became Presiding Elder of the Lancaster District, and had a most successful
year.   But Bishop Turner removed us
from this District and appointed us to
the   pastorate   of   "Mother   Bethel
Church," Philadelphia.   At that time
the present structure was in course of
erection, and so for eight months we
worshipped in Horticultural Hall, on
Broad Street, near Spruce, where we
preached Sabbath after Sabbath, and
paid one hundred dollars each Sunday
for rent.

We stayed at Bethel two years, had

two great revivals and took in over six hundred members. Many of the substantial members that are in Bethel today came in during this time. We finished this church at a cost of fifty-five thousand dollars and raised twenty-eight thousand during the two years' service.

No man stayed at Bethel, during these times, but two years, and even though the church was unanimous for our return, Bishop B. T. Tanner removed us and sent us to Bethel, Wilmington, Delaware. Here we remained two years, had a great revival, assisted by Doctor Benjamin F. Watson, and took in the church, during this revival, two hundred and eighty-four persons. Many of these people are there today, and make some of the leading members of that church. I took in all, four hundred and sixty persons into that church.

After serving here two years, I was

appointed to Harrisburg, Pennsylvania, and finished the new church on State Street, paid the debts, kept up our monthly dues to the Building and Loan Association, and had a balance in bank to meet these dues; but the minister who followed us used up the money in bank and got behind six months in the Building and Loan Association. To save the church the Church Extension Society had to come in and assist him.

In February, 1895, I was appointed by President Grover Cleveland, United States Minister Resident and Consul General to Liberia, West Coast Africa. But we would not agree to take this appointment unless we were permitted to transfer to the Liberia Annual Conference and be given work. We were transferred and made Superintendent of the Liberia Annual Conference, which position we held for four years. We took the money out of our own pocket, purchased the land, and built the first African Methodist Episcopal Church in the city of Monrovia, Liberia. This church stands now as the ELIAS TURNER MEMORIAL

CHAPEL

Up to this time when we held conferences in Monrovia, we had to borrow a church in which to hold them, which was very inconvenient, and we were humiliated more than once by having to wait on a Sunday for a convenient hour to ordain our men; and the finances all went to the borrowed church.

After four years I left Liberia and came to America. I was appointed pastor of Zion Mission, Philadelphia, where I remained one year, renovated the church and paid for it.

At the end of that year, against my will, Bishop W. B. Derrick transferred me to the New York Conference. I was made Presiding Elder of the Long Island District, and had a year of great success; but at the end of that year I asked to be transferred to the Philadelphia Annual Conference, and was appointed to Phoenixville, Pennsylvania, where I remained a few months; yet I never enjoyed a pastorate more than I did the three or four months at Phoenixville.

In August, 1901, Rev. Doctor A. A. Whitman, pastor at Allen Temple, Atlanta, Georgia, died, so Bishop Turner appointed me to Allen Temple by transfer. I served these people for three years, increased their membership, reduced their debts, and enjoyed a pastorate such as I had not for many years. This is a great church, and is now growing to be the equal of any in Georgia.

After three years the quadrennium ended and I had been elected to the General Conference.

GENERAL OFFICER

At this General Conference (1904), I was elected Secretary-Treasurer of the Connectional Preachers' Aid and Mutual Relief Society. Our predecessor had no money in treasury, owed over four or five hundred dollars debts, and the Society had only one hundred and fifty members, none paid up.

He received one thousand dollars salary. We served four years without one cent of salary, paid off all the debts, had one thousand dollars in the treasury at the General Conference. All of our debts were paid to that date, and our membership had grown to seven hundred.

At the end of one quadrennium we were elected Bishop and turned over this department to Rev. W. A. Lewis, having traveled from the Atlantic to the Pacific, the Lakes to the Gulf without salary, selling books, delivering lectures, and riding in "Jim Crow Cars" for thousands of miles each year.

We came to Norfolk, Virginia, in 1908, and our brethren crowned our efforts by electing us one of the Bishops of the African Methodist Episcopal Church, thus ending our ministerial career of thirty-five years as an itinerant as it relates to the pastorate.

The present home of Bishop W. H. Heard,
1426 Rockland St., Phila., Pa.

CHAPTER EIGHT

BISHOPRIC

I had been a member of every General Conference, at every session from 1888, at Indianapolis, Indiana, to this General Conference at Norfolk, Virginia, in 1908, twenty years.

When I was a candidate myself for the Bishopric, I had no support from "the Bench." There were two or three who did not oppose my election, but gave me no support. It was known that Bishops Turner, Gaines, Grant and Smith did all they could for my defeat, but I was elected by a large majority. No man running against me received over fifty-two votes. I received three hundred and seventy-six votes, and was elected one of the Bishops of the A f r i c a n Methodist Episcopal Church and assigned to West Africa.

In January, 1909, with Mrs. Heard

and eight missionaries, I sailed for the West Coast of Africa. We spent a few days in Liverpool and London, England, and then started for the West Coast. After eighteen days' sailing we landed at Sierra Leone, where I held my first conference. This was indeed a great conference for a Mission field.

We left Sierra Leone for Liberia. Here we held our second conference, and our missionaries were all put to work in this field. This brought new life, and after four years' hard work the two conferences were in fine condition, meeting all the obligations incumbent upon them.

Had the war not come, and Bishop Ross been permitted to succeed me, the work would have been far in advance of what it is today.

While I did my best, and all must give me credit for having done great work from the funds at my disposal, yet Bishop Brooks has done the greatest work of any Bishop in our Missionary Fields.   It will go down to his credit, and his name can never be erased from the West Coast.

After eight years' service we were called home, and I was assigned to the Eight Episcopal District, comprising the States of Mississippi and Louisiana. The conference claims of this district, the minutes will show, were not over fifty per cent., but when I reported my fourth round of conferences, I reported ninety per cent. of dollar money, the greatest increase ever reported before, or since. The amount today, 1923, is not equal to what I reported in 1919-20. I did not only financial work, but social and spiritual work as well. The men of the district credit me as a complete success.

Leaving the Eighth District in 1920, we were assigned to the First Episcopal District. The First District reported for 1920, twenty-one thousand seven hundred and eighty dollars and seventy-eight cents Dollar money. We are reporting for this year thirty thousand dollars, which shows our standard financially in Dollar money. We have reported for education this quadrennium more than for four quadrenniums put together, that is, the preceding four quadrenniums to this added together will not amount to the sum total to what we have raised this quadrennium for education.

We are winding up our four years with a membership of more than seven thousand above what we found at the beginning of the quadrennium. The District, to show its appreciation of the work done has just given a reception ending with a great banquet, and a purse of fifteen hundred dollars. This speaks louder than mere words and every conference of its own accord has unanimously voted for the Bishop to be returned to the district for another quadrennium.

From 1908 to 1924 is sixteen years and over this period I have lived much, took many souls into the church, and not shrank from any duty that a Bishop is called upon to fill. I go forth in the name of Him who sent me, "knowing not what may befall me and would not if I could."

CHAPTER NINE

MEN WHO INFLUENCED
MY LIFE

When I was a boy seventeen years of age, the Rev. William J. White, a Baptist preacher of Augusta, Georgia, came to Elberton, my home, as an agent of the Freedmens Bureau, and made a political speech. He was the first colored man I had ever seen who was well educated, and who could use the King's English readily, accurately and convincingly. He very much influenced me and I determined from that night to be a MAN, and to fill an important place in life's arena.

It was just the dawn of political awakening for the Negro. The Democrats that night tarred his horse all over with pitch, but the next morning he was up, had his horse attended to, hitched him to his buggy and went on his errand. I knew him for many years afterwards. He edited a paper called, "The Georgia Baptist." He was always outspoken for Orthodox Religion and for the Republican Party.

In January, 1867, I had an opportunity to go to Augusta, Georgia, and there for the first time I heard Bishop H. M. Turner speak. He spoke on "The Negro in All Ages."

He spoke for two hours. I was so impressed with the pictures and historic facts he presented of the Race in the past ages, and of the men of the present, that my life is largely what it is because of the impressions made at this meeting.

I returned to my home in Elberton, and began my future work. The Rev. Aaron Harris was presiding Elder of the C. M. E. Church (Colored Methodist Episcopal Church), at Elberton, and had me as secretary of the Official

Board and Quarterly Conference in the
C. M. E. Church before I was a Christian.

Bishop Vanderhorst, of that Church,
came to Elberton and preached. I was
greatly impressed by his sermon, and
being secretary of the Official Board
and Quarterly Conference, I determined to be a Christian, and fill important
places in the Church and in social life.

A. M. E. GALLEY K

At Athens, Georgia, I taught in the
A. M. E. Church. The Rev. Richard
Harper, a medical graduate, was the
pastor. He was a good preacher and
his sermons greatly influenced me.

After he was removed from Athens
the Rev. Lawrence Thomas took charge
of the Church. His sermons, lectures,
and life impressed me to emulate and
imitate, if possible, his life.

Bishop Gaines, also, though not so
well educated, influenced me to greater
activity in the ministry.

When I joined the Annual Conference, Bishop Jabez Pitt Campbell was the Presiding Bishop. He was a great gospel preacher and I made him my ideal. Bishops Shorter, Ward, and Dickerson influenced me more than any men in the A. M. E. Church, except Bishop Turner.

These men were personally concerned in my advancement, and helped me by word and action, and I am greatly indebted to all of them. They put in me determination, courage and enthusiasm, and, I can say, had I not been under the influence of the Bishops named, perhaps I would not be what I am today.

Politically, Honorable Robert Brown Elliott and Bishop Richard Harvey Cain, who spoke so manfully on the "Civil Rights Bill," made me a greater advocate of the rights of my people than I would have been. I was also influenced by Congressman Robert Smalls and the Honorable Thomas Miller, of Beaufort, South Carolina.

Thus I became a staunch Republican by the speeches delivered in Congress by these men.

The reply of Mr. Elliott to the Honorable B. H. Hill, of Georgia, is a masterpiece. No man can read it and not side with the argument he produced in favor of the Negro.

The Rev. J. C. Price, of the A. M. E. Zion Church, lectured for me several times and spent much time in my home. He was one of the most eloquent and logical platform orators of his day.

The Honorable Frederick Douglass also spoke in my church and lived in my home, and he influenced my life for the uplift of humanity, and for the advancement of the Race.

I cannot name all the men who helped me in one way or another, but those mentioned helped me most.

I saw in the lives of Professor H. T.

Kealing, Professor John R. Hawkins, and Professor A. S. Jackson, laymen who have done so much for the Church on the platform that they greatly encouraged me.

The speeches and sermons of Bishop J. C. Embry and Rev. William Decker Johnson, of Georgia (not Bishop Johnson) who was Secretary of Education, also helped me.

And when I went to Liberia and met a Negro President and Cabinet, I was so impressed that the Negro had a future, that I determined to spend my life in trying to brighten that future.

In 1882 I married my second wife, Miss Josie D. Henderson, of Charlotte, North Carolina. She is scholarly and poetic, and her use of the English language, as well as the criticism of my sermons, have done much in making me the preacher they say I am.

My present secretary, Rev. H. H. Cooper, Director of the Drive, is a man who carefully and correctly uses the language we speak, and I have gotten, and get, impressions and information from him.

On New Year's Eve night, 1923, I heard a sermon by Rev. W. S. Drummond, Presiding Elder. The language could be criticised, but the thought and delivery were superb.

I could continue this line of description, but suffice it to say: I get lessons from any and all who drop a word worth while.

CHAPTER TEN

THE LIFE OF WILLIAM H. HEARD

An Original Poem
BY
EPHRAIM D. TYLER
Shreveport, Louisiana

With delight and perfect pleasure
I would gladly speak a word,
About this famous character,
This great Bishop, William Heard,
All aboard the time's excursion,
Ride this train of thought with me,
To the year eighteen and fifty,
In the nineteenth century.
Tarry here a single moment
Though the time is fleeting fast,
Till I paint a mental picture
Of an event of the past.

Yonder mid the hills of Georgia,
Elbert County's farming land,
Let us seek the first location
Where my narrative began.
To a lowly little Cabin,
Just a slave hut let us go,
Where there were no lovely flowers,
Blooming near the peasants' door.
Just a lowly little Cabin,
With an old hay mattress bed,
With rough riven boards for roofing,
And no ceiling overhead.

Just a lowly little Cabin,
A dark, lonely hut at night,
Where at times perhaps a pine knot
Was the only source of light.
Just a lowly little Cabin,
Home of sorrows, griefs and cares,
Where true Christians knelt at bedtime
To present their evening prayer.
Just a lowly little Cabin,
With but little joy or mirth,
Where the housewife baked her corn pone
With the embers 'round the hearth.

Just a lowly little Cabin,
But, my visions are too faint,
Use your own imagination,
Take your own paint brush and paint.
Once when all the dusky shadows
Of the night had passed away,
When the golden rays of sunshine
Brought to man a bright new day;
When horns blew upon plantations,
Calling slaves to service hours,
When the crystal dewdrops sparkled
On the grass and fragrant flowers.

When the little birds sat singing
In the branches of the trees,
And the sweetness of their music
Wafted through the balmy breeze.
When proud Anglo-Saxon children
Took their books and marched to school,

And the Negro peasant farm boy
Tilled the soil behind his mule;
When small children of this family
Were rushed out of doors to play,
To Heard's lowly little Cabin
Came a visitor one day.

Just a tender little infant,
Filled a mother's heart with joy
That she had become the parent
Of a lovely baby boy.
Just a tender little infant,
With bright eyes and smiling face,
Gave to men a hopeful prospect
Of a leader for my race.
Just a tender little infant,
Nestled in its mother's breast,
While the silver queen moved slowly
Towards the distant pale blue west.

Just a tender little infant,
Reason with me if you can,
Gave hopes to a Christian mother
Of a useful future man.
Just a tender little infant,
Who was born a lowly slave,
Started out upon life's journey,
From the cradle to the grave.
When a few short days passed over,
An important question came,
When somebody asked the mother
What would be the baby's name.

But this question was decided,
And was answered with a word
When the mother frankly stated
She would call him William Heard.
I could spend the next half hour
Telling you of little Bill,
And you would know very little
Of his early childhood still.
But time, like a fleeting shadow,
Comes to us and then 'tis gone,
I must mention youth and manhood—
Let us hasten briefly on.

It was seen that little William
Had a literary crave,
In the noon tide of his boyhood,
Even though an humble slave.
The next stop for time's excursion,
At which we shall now arrive,
Is Negro Emancipation,
Eighteen hundred sixty-five,
When the fingers of Abe Lincoln
Firmly grasped the writing pen,
To give liberty and freedom
To the sons of Negro men.

When God's time had come to answer
Faithful Christian mothers' prayers,
Some of which had been presented
For more than two hundred years.
When the Curse of slavery ended
With triumphant shouts of joy,

The Heard family decided
They would educate their boy.
In the common schools of Georgia
William learned to read and write,
And prepared his daily lessons
With the greatest of delight.

He was apt in every study,
Had a splendid memory.
When he left high school he entered
The Clark University.
To South Carolina and Atlanta
Universities he went,
In pursuit of education
Many faithful years were spent.
The Episcopal Reform School
Of Philadelphia took a hand
In building this mental structure,
To make Heard a Noble man.

After years of preparation
To fill some exalted place,
Heard spent twelve years in the schoolroom
With the children of his race.
Then he spent three years in service
As a Railway Postal Clerk,
From the sacred task of duty
He was never known to shirk.
For one term in South Carolina
This meek peasant of my race
Was member of the Legislature;
Few men could have filled his place

Minister and Consul General,
Heard four years of service spent,
Under Mr. Grover Cleveland,
Then the nation's President.
In Liberia and Africa,
From what we can understand,
As a Minister and General,
William Heard was quite a man.
As a statesman of this country
Heard had many things in view,
But God showed him broader visions
Of much greater work to do.

In the year of eighteen eighty,
Willingly Heard gave up all
To devote his time and talent
To his Ministerial call.
He served first at Johnstown Mission
In his earlier manhood,
And the whole town of Atlanta
Said the Minister made good.
Then he served Markham Street Mission,
Where he stood a rigid test,
But in every case his service
Proved to be the very best.

Men of Aiken, South Carolina,
In Markham Street Mission Church,
Say no other man on record
Has improved their lives so much.
The next charge, Mt. Zion Station,
Was a battle to be won,

And Charleston, South Carolina,
Said the job was neatly done.
Being sent to Allen Chapel,
Very soon he came in touch,
And became the famous pastor
Of the Mother Bethel Church.

In the town of Philadelphia
Heard's success was great indeed;
He was made Presiding Elder,
Proving Worthiness to lead.
Preachers of Lancaster District
Under Heard worked in accord,
Harrisburg gave him a record,
After which he went abroad.
He was then the Superintendent
Of Africa's Western Coast,
Where he made a reputation
Of which but few men can boast.

He next served at Zion Chapel,
Philadelphia's Negro pride,
And on to Long Island district,
New York Conference to preside.
He became the Secretary
Of A. M. E. Preachers' Aid;
For four years he gave his service,
And no salary was paid.
I must tell you in conclusion,
Heard's accomplishments were great,
And he was elected Bishop
In the May of nineteen eight.

For eight years of splendid service
Upon Africa's West Coast,
With untiring faith and courage
Bishop Heard stood at his post.
I would give you a brief outline
Of his work for forty years,
But there's too much territory,
Too much service, too much tears.
God has given us this great life
Of true service on the earth,
We have learned to love him dearly,
We appreciate his worth.

Bishop Heard has preached the Gospe
Over sea and over land,
He is now Presiding Bishop
Where his great church first began.
He resides in Philadelphia,
Lives a peaceful, happy life,
And attribtues his great success
To a useful, faithful wife.
To God be Praise and Glory
For this Man to preach His Word,
For my race has found a leader.
In this Bishop William Heard.

DUE

PRINTED IN U.S.A.